Supplements to

A

Course in

Miracles

Supplements to

A

Course in

Miracles

P S Y C H O T H E R A P Y
Purpose, Process and Practice

T H E   S O N G   O F   P R A Y E R
Prayer, Forgiveness, Healing

F O U N D A T I O N   F O R   I N N E R   P E A C E
V I K I N G

VIKING
Published by the Penguin Group
Penguin Books USA Inc., 375 Hudson Street, New York, New York 10014, U.S.A.
Penguin Books Ltd, 27 Wrights Lane, London W8 5TZ, England
Penguin Books Australia Ltd, Ringwood, Victoria, Australia
Penguin Books Canada Ltd, 10 Alcorn Avenue, Toronto, Ontario, Canada M4V 3B2
Penguin Books (N.Z.) Ltd, 182–190 Wairau Road, Auckland 10, New Zealand

Penguin Books Ltd, Registered Offices: Harmondsworth, Middlesex, England

Published in 1996 by Viking Penguin,
a division of Penguin Books USA Inc.

3 5 7 9 10 8 6 4 2

Previously published as two pamphlets by the Foundation for Inner Peace.
ISBN 0-670-86994-5
CIP data is available from the Library of Congress.

This book is printed on acid-free paper. ∞

Printed in the United States of America
Set in Granjon

PSYCHOTHERAPY

Purpose, Process and Practice

An Extension of the Principles of

A Course in Miracles

SECOND EDITION

CONTENTS

PSYCHOTHERAPY

Purpose, Process and Practice

INTRODUCTION

1. Psychotherapy is the only form of therapy there is. ²Since only the mind can be sick, only the mind can be healed. ³Only the mind is in need of healing. ⁴This does not appear to be the case, for the manifestations of this world seem real indeed. ⁵Psychotherapy is necessary so that an individual can begin to question their reality. ⁶Sometimes he is able to start to open his mind without formal help, but even then it is always some change in his perception of interpersonal relationships that enables him to do so. ⁷Sometimes he needs a more structured, extended relationship with an "official" therapist. ⁸Either way, the task is the same; the patient must be helped to change his mind about the "reality" of illusions.

1

THE PURPOSE
OF PSYCHOTHERAPY

1. Very simply, the purpose of psychotherapy is to remove the blocks to truth. ²Its aim is to aid the patient in abandoning his fixed delusional system, and to begin to reconsider the spurious cause and effect relationships on which it rests. ³No one in this world escapes fear, but everyone can reconsider its causes and learn to evaluate them correctly. ⁴God has given everyone a Teacher Whose wisdom and help far exceed whatever contributions an earthly therapist can provide. ⁵Yet there are times and situations in which an earthly patient-therapist relationship becomes the means through which He offers His greater gifts to both.

2. What better purpose could any relationship have than to invite the Holy Spirit to enter into it and give it His

1. THE PURPOSE OF PSYCHOTHERAPY

Own great gift of rejoicing? ²What higher goal could there be for anyone than to learn to call upon God and hear His Answer? ³And what more transcendent aim can there be than to recall the way, the truth and the life, and to remember God? ⁴To help in this is the proper purpose of psychotherapy. ⁵Could anything be holier? ⁶For psychotherapy, correctly understood, teaches forgiveness and helps the patient to recognize and accept it. ⁷And in his healing is the therapist forgiven with him.

3. Everyone who needs help, regardless of the form of his distress, is attacking himself, and his peace of mind is suffering in consequence. ²These tendencies are often described as "self-destructive," and the patient often regards them in that way himself. ³What he does not realize and needs to learn is that this "self," which can attack and be attacked as well, is a concept he made up. ⁴Further, he cherishes it, defends it, and is sometimes even willing to "sacrifice" his "life" on its behalf. ⁵For he regards it as himself. ⁶This self he sees as being acted on, reacting to external forces as they demand, and helpless midst the power of the world.

4. Psychotherapy, then, must restore to his awareness the ability to make his own decisions. ²He must become willing to reverse his thinking, and to understand that what

he thought projected its effects on him were made by his projections on the world. ³The world he sees does therefore not exist. ⁴Until this is at least in part accepted, the patient cannot see himself as really capable of making decisions. ⁵And he will fight against his freedom because he thinks that it is slavery.

5. The patient need not think of truth as God in order to make progress in salvation. ²But he must begin to separate truth from illusion, recognizing that they are not the same, and becoming increasingly willing to see illusions as false and to accept the truth as true. ³His Teacher will take him on from there, as far as he is ready to go. ⁴Psychotherapy can only save him time. ⁵The Holy Spirit uses time as He thinks best, and He is never wrong. ⁶Psychotherapy under His direction is one of the means He uses to save time, and to prepare additional teachers for His work. ⁷There is no end to the help that He begins and He directs. ⁸By whatever routes He chooses, all psychotherapy leads to God in the end. ⁹But that is up to Him. ¹⁰We are all His psychotherapists, for He would have us all be healed in Him.

2

THE PROCESS
OF PSYCHOTHERAPY

Introduction

1. Psychotherapy is a process that changes the view of the self. [2]At best this "new" self is a more beneficent self-concept, but psychotherapy can hardly be expected to establish reality. [3]That is not its function. [4]If it can make way for reality, it has achieved its ultimate success. [5]Its whole function, in the end, is to help the patient deal with one fundamental error; the belief that anger brings him something he really wants, and that by justifying attack he is protecting himself. [6]To whatever extent he comes to realize that this is an error, to that extent is he truly saved.

2. Patients do not enter the therapeutic relationship with this goal in mind. [2]On the contrary, such concepts mean little to them, or they would not need help. [3]Their aim is to be able to retain their self-concept exactly as it is, but

without the suffering that it entails. [4]Their whole equilibrium rests on the insane belief that this is possible. [5]And because to the sane mind it is so clearly impossible, what they seek is magic. [6]In illusions the impossible is easily accomplished, but only at the cost of making illusions true. [7]The patient has already paid this price. [8]Now he wants a "better" illusion.

3. At the beginning, then, the patient's goal and the therapist's are at variance. [2]The therapist as well as the patient may cherish false self-concepts, but their respective perceptions of "improvement" still must differ. [3]The patient hopes to learn how to get the changes he wants without changing his self-concept to any significant extent. [4]He hopes, in fact, to stabilize it sufficiently to include within it the magical powers he seeks in psychotherapy. [5]He wants to make the vulnerable invulnerable and the finite limitless. [6]The self he sees is his god, and he seeks only to serve it better.

4. Regardless of how sincere the therapist himself may be, he must want to change the patient's self-concept in some way that he believes is real. [2]The task of therapy is one of reconciling these differences. [3]Hopefully, both will learn to give up their original goals, for it is only in relationships that salvation can be found. [4]At the beginning, it is inev-

itable that patients and therapists alike accept unrealistic goals not completely free of magical overtones. [5]They are finally given up in the minds of both.

I. The Limits on Psychotherapy

1. Yet the ideal outcome is rarely achieved. [2]Therapy begins with the realization that healing is of the mind, and in psychotherapy those have come together who already believe this. [3]It may be they will not get much further, for no one learns beyond his own readiness. [4]Yet levels of readiness change, and when therapist or patient has reached the next one, there will be a relationship held out to them that meets the changing need. [5]Perhaps they will come together again and advance in the same relationship, making it holier. [6]Or perhaps each of them will enter into another commitment. [7]Be assured of this; each will progress. [8]Retrogression is temporary. [9]The overall direction is one of progress toward the truth.

2. Psychotherapy itself cannot be creative. [2]This is one of the errors which the ego fosters; that it is capable of true change, and therefore of true creativity. [3]When we speak of "the saving illusion" or "the final dream," this is not

what we mean, but here is the ego's last defense. [4]"Resistance" is its way of looking at things; its interpretation of progress and growth. [5]These interpretations will be wrong of necessity, because they are delusional. [6]The changes the ego seeks to make are not really changes. [7]They are but deeper shadows, or perhaps different cloud patterns. [8]Yet what is made of nothingness cannot be called new or different. [9]Illusions are illusions; truth is truth.

3. Resistance as defined here can be characteristic of a therapist as well as of a patient. [2]Either way, it sets a limit on psychotherapy because it restricts its aims. [3]Nor can the Holy Spirit fight against the intrusions of the ego on the therapeutic process. [4]But He will wait, and His patience is infinite. [5]His goal is wholly undivided always. [6]Whatever resolutions patient and therapist reach in connection with their own divergent goals, they cannot become completely reconciled as one until they join with His. [7]Only then is all conflict over, for only then can there be certainty.

4. Ideally, psychotherapy is a series of holy encounters in which brothers meet to bless each other and to receive the peace of God. [2]And this will one day come to pass for every "patient" on the face of this earth, for who except a patient could possibly have come here? [3]The therapist is

only a somewhat more specialized teacher of God. [4]He learns through teaching, and the more advanced he is the more he teaches and the more he learns. [5]But whatever stage he is in, there are patients who need him just that way. [6]They cannot take more than he can give for now. [7]Yet both will find sanity at last.

II. The Place of Religion in Psychotherapy

1. To be a teacher of God, it is not necessary to be religious or even to believe in God to any recognizable extent. [2]It is necessary, however, to teach forgiveness rather than condemnation. [3]Even in this, complete consistency is not required, for one who had achieved that point could teach salvation completely, within an instant and without a word. [4]Yet he who has learned all things does not need a teacher, and the healed have no need for a therapist. [5]Relationships are still the temple of the Holy Spirit, and they will be made perfect in time and restored to eternity.

2. Formal religion has no place in psychotherapy, but it also has no real place in religion. [2]In this world, there is an astonishing tendency to join contradictory words into one

term without perceiving the contradiction at all. ³The attempt to formalize religion is so obviously an ego attempt to reconcile the irreconcilable that it hardly requires elaboration here. ⁴Religion is experience; psychotherapy is experience. ⁵At the highest levels they become one. ⁶Neither is truth itself, but both can lead to truth. ⁷What can be necessary to find truth, which remains perfectly obvious, but to remove the seeming obstacles to true awareness?

3. No one who learns to forgive can fail to remember God. ²Forgiveness, then, is all that need be taught, because it is all that need be learned. ³All blocks to the remembrance of God are forms of unforgiveness, and nothing else. ⁴This is never apparent to the patient, and only rarely so to the therapist. ⁵The world has marshalled all its forces against this one awareness, for in it lies the ending of the world and all it stands for.

4. Yet it is not the awareness of God that constitutes a reasonable goal for psychotherapy. ²This will come when psychotherapy is complete, for where there is forgiveness truth must come. ³It would be unfair indeed if belief in God were necessary to psychotherapeutic success. ⁴Nor is belief in God a really meaningful concept, for God can be but known. ⁵Belief implies that unbelief is possible, but knowledge of God has no true opposite. ⁶Not to know

God is to have no knowledge, and it is to this that all un-forgiveness leads. ⁷And without knowledge one can have only belief.

5. Different teaching aids appeal to different people. ²Some forms of religion have nothing to do with God, and some forms of psychotherapy have nothing to do with healing. ³Yet if pupil and teacher join in sharing one goal, God will enter into their relationship because He has been invited to come in. ⁴In the same way, a union of purpose between patient and therapist restores the place of God to ascendance, first through Christ's vision and then through the memory of God Himself. ⁵The process of psychotherapy is the return to sanity. ⁶Teacher and pupil, therapist and patient, are all insane or they would not be here. ⁷Together they can find a pathway out, for no one will find sanity alone.

6. If healing is an invitation to God to enter into His Kingdom, what difference does it make how the invitation is written? ²Does the paper matter, or the ink, or the pen? ³Or is it he who writes that gives the invitation? ⁴God comes to those who would restore His world, for they have found the way to call to Him. ⁵If any two are joined, He must be there. ⁶It does not matter what their purpose is, but they must share it wholly to succeed. ⁷It is

impossible to share a goal not blessed by Christ, for what is unseen through His eyes is too fragmented to be meaningful.

7. As true religion heals, so must true psychotherapy be religious. ²But both have many forms, because no good teacher uses one approach to every pupil. ³On the contrary, he listens patiently to each one, and lets him formulate his own curriculum; not the curriculum's goal, but how he can best reach the aim it sets for him. ⁴Perhaps the teacher does not think of God as part of teaching. ⁵Perhaps the psychotherapist does not understand that healing comes from God. ⁶They can succeed where many who believe they have found God will fail.

8. What must the teacher do to ensure learning? ²What must the therapist do to bring healing about? ³Only one thing; the same requirement salvation asks of everyone. ⁴Each one must share one goal with someone else, and in so doing, lose all sense of separate interests. ⁵Only by doing this is it possible to transcend the narrow boundaries the ego would impose upon the self. ⁶Only by doing this can teacher and pupil, therapist and patient, you and I, accept Atonement and learn to give it as it was received.

9. Communion is impossible alone. ²No one who stands apart can receive Christ's vision. ³It is held out to him, but

he cannot hold out his hand to receive it. ⁴Let him be still and recognize his brother's need is his own. ⁵And let him then meet his brother's need as his and see that they are met as one, for such they are. ⁶What is religion but an aid in helping him to see that this is so? ⁷And what is psychotherapy except a help in just this same direction? ⁸It is the goal that makes these processes the same, for they are one in purpose and must thus be one in means.

III. The Role of the Psychotherapist

1. The psychotherapist is a leader in the sense that he walks slightly ahead of the patient, and helps him to avoid a few of the pitfalls along the road by seeing them first. ²Ideally, he is also a follower, for One should walk ahead of him to give him light to see. ³Without this One, both will merely stumble blindly on to nowhere. ⁴It is, however, impossible that this One be wholly absent if the goal is healing. ⁵He may, however, not be recognized. ⁶And so the little light that can be then accepted is all there is to light the way to truth.

2. Healing is limited by the limitations of the psychother-

apist, as it is limited by those of the patient. [2]The aim of the process, therefore, is to transcend these limits. [3]Neither can do this alone, but when they join, the potentiality for transcending all limitations has been given them. [4]Now the extent of their success depends on how much of this potentiality they are willing to use. [5]The willingness may come from either one at the beginning, and as the other shares it, it will grow. [6]Progress becomes a matter of decision; it can reach almost to Heaven or go no further than a step or two from hell.

3. It is quite possible for psychotherapy to seem to fail. [2]It is even possible for the result to look like retrogression. [3]But in the end there must be some success. [4]One asks for help; another hears and tries to answer in the form of help. [5]This is the formula for salvation, and must heal. [6]Divided goals alone can interfere with perfect healing. [7]One wholly egoless therapist could heal the world without a word, merely by being there. [8]No one need see him or talk to him or even know of his existence. [9]His simple Presence is enough to heal.

4. The ideal therapist is one with Christ. [2]But healing is a process, not a fact. [3]The therapist cannot progress without the patient, and the patient cannot be ready to receive the Christ or he could not be sick. [4]In a sense, the egoless

psychotherapist is an abstraction that stands at the end of the process of healing, too advanced to believe in sickness and too near to God to keep his feet on earth. ⁵Now he can help through those in need of help, for thus he carries out the plan established for salvation. ⁶The psychotherapist becomes his patient, working through other patients to express his thoughts as he receives them from the Mind of Christ.

IV. The Process of Illness

1. As all therapy is psychotherapy, so all illness is mental illness. ²It is a judgment on the Son of God, and judgment is a mental activity. ³Judgment is a decision, made again and again, against creation and its Creator. ⁴It is a decision to perceive the universe as you would have created it. ⁵It is a decision that truth can lie and must be lies. ⁶What, then, can illness be except an expression of sorrow and of guilt? ⁷And who could weep but for his innocence?

2. Once God's Son is seen as guilty, illness becomes inevitable. ²It has been asked for and will be received. ³And all who ask for illness have now condemned themselves to seek for remedies that cannot help, because their faith is

in the illness and not in salvation. [4]There can be nothing that a change of mind cannot effect, for all external things are only shadows of a decision already made. [5]Change the decision, and how can its shadow be unchanged? [6]Illness can be but guilt's shadow, grotesque and ugly since it mimics deformity. [7]If a deformity is seen as real, what could its shadow be except deformed?

3. The descent into hell follows step by step in an inevitable course, once the decision that guilt is real has been made. [2]Sickness and death and misery now stalk the earth in unrelenting waves, sometimes together and sometimes in grim succession. [3]Yet all these things, however real they seem, are but illusions. [4]Who could have faith in them once this is realized? [5]And who could not have faith in them until he realizes this? [6]Healing is therapy or correction, and we have said already and will say again, all therapy is psychotherapy. [7]To heal the sick is but to bring this realization to them.

4. The word "cure" has come into disrepute among the more "respectable" therapists of the world, and justly so. [2]For not one of them can cure, and not one of them understands healing. [3]At worst, they but make the body real in their own minds, and having done so, seek for magic by which to heal the ills with which their minds endow it.

⁴How could such a process cure? ⁵It is ridiculous from start to finish. ⁶Yet having started, it must finish thus. ⁷It is as if God were the devil and must be found in evil. ⁸How could love be there? ⁹And how could sickness cure? ¹⁰Are not these both one question?

5. At best, and the word is perhaps questionable here, the "healers" of the world may recognize the mind as the source of illness. ²But their error lies in the belief that it can cure itself. ³This has some merit in a world where "degrees of error" is a meaningful concept. ⁴Yet must their cures remain temporary, or another illness rise instead, for death has not been overcome until the meaning of love is understood. ⁵And who can understand this without the Word of God, given by Him to the Holy Spirit as His gift to you?

6. Illness of any kind may be defined as the result of a view of the self as weak, vulnerable, evil and endangered, and thus in need of constant defense. ²Yet if such were really the self, defense would be impossible. ³Therefore, the defenses sought for must be magical. ⁴They must overcome all limits perceived in the self, at the same time making a new self-concept into which the old one cannot return. ⁵In a word, error is accepted as real and dealt with by illusions. ⁶Truth being brought to illusions, reality now be-

comes a threat and is perceived as evil. [7]Love becomes feared because reality is love. [8]Thus is the circle closed against the "in-roads" of salvation.

7. Illness is therefore a mistake and needs correction. [2]And as we have already emphasized, correction cannot be achieved by first establishing the "rightness" of the mistake and then overlooking it. [3]If illness is real it cannot be overlooked in truth, for to overlook reality is insanity. [4]Yet that is magic's purpose; to make illusions true through false perception. [5]This cannot heal, for it opposes truth. [6]Perhaps an illusion of health is substituted for a little while, but not for long. [7]Fear cannot long be hidden by illusions, for it is part of them. [8]It will escape and take another form, being the source of all illusions.

8. Sickness is insanity because all sickness is mental illness, and in it there are no degrees. [2]One of the illusions by which sickness is perceived as real is the belief that illness varies in intensity; that the degree of threat differs according to the form it takes. [3]Herein lies the basis of all errors, for all of them are but attempts to compromise by seeing just a little bit of hell. [4]This is a mockery so alien to God that it must be forever inconceivable. [5]But the insane believe it because they are insane.

9. A madman will defend his own illusions because in

them he sees his own salvation. ²Thus, he will attack the one who tries to save him from them, believing that he is attacking him. ³This curious circle of attack-defense is one of the most difficult problems with which the psychotherapist must deal. ⁴In fact, this is his central task; the core of psychotherapy. ⁵The therapist is seen as one who is attacking the patient's most cherished possession; his picture of himself. ⁶And since this picture has become the patient's security as he perceives it, the therapist cannot but be seen as a real source of danger, to be attacked and even killed.

10. The psychotherapist, then, has a tremendous responsibility. ²He must meet attack without attack, and therefore without defense. ³It is his task to demonstrate that defenses are not necessary, and that defenselessness is strength. ⁴This must be his teaching, if his lesson is to be that sanity is safe. ⁵It cannot be too strongly emphasized that the insane believe that sanity is threat. ⁶This is the corollary of the "original sin"; the belief that guilt is real and fully justified. ⁷It is therefore the psychotherapist's function to teach that guilt, being unreal, cannot be justified. ⁸But neither is it safe. ⁹And thus it must remain unwanted as well as unreal.

11. Salvation's single doctrine is the goal of all therapy.

²Relieve the mind of the insane burden of guilt it carries so wearily, and healing is accomplished. ³The body is not cured. ⁴It is merely recognized as what it is. ⁵Seen rightly, its purpose can be understood. ⁶What is the need for sickness then? ⁷Given this single shift, all else will follow. ⁸There is no need for complicated change. ⁹There is no need for long analyses and wearying discussion and pursuits. ¹⁰The truth is simple, being one for all.

V. The Process of Healing

1. While truth is simple, it must still be taught to those who have already lost their way in endless mazes of complexity. ²This is the great illusion. ³In its wake comes the inevitable belief that, to be safe, one must control the unknown. ⁴This strange belief relies on certain steps which never reach to consciousness. ⁵First, it is ushered in by the belief that there are forces to be overcome to be alive at all. ⁶And next, it seems as if these forces can be held at bay only by an inflated sense of self that holds in darkness what is truly felt, and seeks to raise illusions to the light. 2. Let us remember that the ones who come to us for help are bitterly afraid. ²What they believe will help can only

harm; what they believe will harm alone can help. ³Prog-
ress becomes impossible until the patient is persuaded to
reverse his twisted way of looking at the world; his
twisted way of looking at himself. ⁴The truth is simple.
⁵Yet it must be taught to those who think it will endanger
them. ⁶It must be taught to those who will attack because
they feel endangered, and to those who need the lesson of
defenselessness above all else, to show them what is
strength.

3. If this world were ideal, there could perhaps be ideal
therapy. ²And yet it would be useless in an ideal state. ³We
speak of ideal teaching in a world in which the perfect
teacher could not long remain; the perfect psychotherapist
is but a glimmer of a thought not yet conceived. ⁴But still
we speak of what can yet be done in helping the insane
within the bounds of the attainable. ⁵While they are sick,
they can and must be helped. ⁶No more than that is asked
of psychotherapy; no less than all he has to give is worthy
of the therapist. ⁷For God Himself holds out his brother
as his savior from the world.

4. Healing is holy. ²Nothing in the world is holier than
helping one who asks for help. ³And two come very close
to God in this attempt, however limited, however lacking
in sincerity. ⁴Where two have joined for healing, God is

there. ⁵And He has guaranteed that He will hear and answer them in truth. ⁶They can be sure that healing is a process He directs, because it is according to His Will. ⁷We have His Word to guide us, as we try to help our brothers. ⁸Let us not forget that we are helpless of ourselves, and lean upon a strength beyond our little scope for what to teach as well as what to learn.

5. A brother seeking aid can bring us gifts beyond the heights perceived in any dream. ²He offers us salvation, for he comes to us as Christ and Savior. ³What he asks is asked by God through him. ⁴And what we do for him becomes the gift we give to God. ⁵The sacred calling of God's holy Son for help in his perceived distress can be but answered by his Father. ⁶Yet He needs a voice through which to speak His holy Word; a hand to reach His Son and touch his heart. ⁷In such a process, who could not be healed? ⁸This holy interaction is the plan of God Himself, by which His Son is saved.

6. For two have joined. ²And now God's promises are kept by Him. ³The limits laid on both the patient and the therapist will count as nothing, for the healing has begun. ⁴What they must start their Father will complete. ⁵For He has never asked for more than just the smallest willingness, the least advance, the tiniest of whispers of His

Name. [6]To ask for help, whatever form it takes, is but to call on Him. [7]And He will send His Answer through the therapist who best can serve His Son in all his present needs. [8]Perhaps the answer does not seem to be a gift from Heaven. [9]It may even seem to be a worsening and not a help. [10]Yet let the outcome not be judged by us.

7. Somewhere all gifts of God must be received. [2]In time no effort can be made in vain. [3]It is not our perfection that is asked in our attempts to heal. [4]We are deceived already, if we think there is a need of healing. [5]And the truth will come to us only through one who seems to share our dream of sickness. [6]Let us help him to forgive himself for all the trespasses with which he would condemn himself without a cause. [7]His healing is our own. [8]And as we see the sinlessness in him come shining through the veil of guilt that shrouds the Son of God, we will behold in him the face of Christ, and understand that it is but our own.

8. Let us stand silently before God's Will, and do what it has chosen that we do. [2]There is one way alone by which we come to where all dreams began. [3]And it is there that we will lay them down, to come away in peace forever. [4]Hear a brother call for help and answer him. [5]It will be God to Whom you answer, for you called on Him. [6]There is no other way to hear His Voice. [7]There is no other way

to seek His Son. [8]There is no other way to find your Self. [9]Holy is healing, for the Son of God returns to Heaven through its kind embrace. [10]For healing tells him, in the Voice for God, that all his sins have been forgiven him.

VI. The Definition of Healing

1. The process of psychotherapy, then, can be defined simply as forgiveness, for no healing can be anything else. [2]The unforgiving are sick, believing they are unforgiven. [3]The hanging-on to guilt, its hugging-close and sheltering, its loving protection and alert defense,—all this is but the grim refusal to forgive. [4]"God may not enter here" the sick repeat, over and over, while they mourn their loss and yet rejoice in it. [5]Healing occurs as a patient begins to hear the dirge he sings, and questions its validity. [6]Until he hears it, he cannot understand that it is he who sings it to himself. [7]To hear it is the first step in recovery. [8]To question it must then become his choice.

2. There is a tendency, and it is very strong, to hear this song of death only an instant, and then dismiss it uncorrected. [2]These fleeting awarenesses represent the many opportunities given us literally "to change our tune." [3]The

sound of healing can be heard instead. ⁴But first the willingness to question the "truth" of the song of condemnation must arise. ⁵The strange distortions woven inextricably into the self-concept, itself but a pseudo-creation, make this ugly sound seem truly beautiful. ⁶"The rhythm of the universe," "the herald angel's song," all these and more are heard instead of loud discordant shrieks.

3. The ear translates; it does not hear. ²The eye reproduces; it does not see. ³Their task is to make agreeable whatever is called on, however disagreeable it may be. ⁴They answer the decisions of the mind, reproducing its desires and translating them into acceptable and pleasant forms. ⁵Sometimes the thought behind the form breaks through, but only very briefly, and the mind grows fearful and begins to doubt its sanity. ⁶Yet it will not permit its slaves to change the forms they look upon; the sounds they hear. ⁷These are its "remedies"; its "safeguards" from insanity.

4. These testimonies which the senses bring have but one purpose; to justify attack and thus keep unforgiveness unrecognized for what it is. ²Seen undisguised it is intolerable. ³Without protection it could not endure. ⁴Here is all sickness cherished, but without the recognition that this is so. ⁵For when an unforgiveness is not recognized, the form it takes seems to be something else. ⁶And now it is

the "something else" that seems to terrify. ⁷But it is not the "something else" that can be healed. ⁸It is not sick, and needs no remedy. ⁹To concentrate your healing efforts here is but futility. ¹⁰Who can cure what cannot be sick and make it well?

5. Sickness takes many forms, and so does unforgiveness. ²The forms of one but reproduce the forms of the other, for they are the same illusion. ³So closely is one translated into the other, that a careful study of the form a sickness takes will point quite clearly to the form of unforgiveness that it represents. ⁴Yet seeing this will not effect a cure. ⁵That is achieved by only one recognition; that only forgiveness heals an unforgiveness, and only an unforgiveness can possibly give rise to sickness of any kind.

6. This realization is the final goal of psychotherapy. ²How is it reached? ³The therapist sees in the patient all that he has not forgiven in himself, and is thus given another chance to look at it, open it to re-evaluation and forgive it. ⁴When this occurs, he sees his sins as gone into a past that is no longer here. ⁵Until he does this, he must think of evil as besetting him here and now. ⁶The patient is his screen for the projection of his sins, enabling him to let them go. ⁷Let him retain one spot of sin in what he looks upon, and his release is partial and will not be sure.

7. No one is healed alone. ²This is the joyous song salvation sings to all who hear its Voice. ³This statement cannot be too often remembered by all who see themselves as therapists. ⁴Their patients can but be seen as the bringers of forgiveness, for it is they who come to demonstrate their sinlessness to eyes that still believe that sin is there to look upon. ⁵Yet will the proof of sinlessness, seen in the patient and accepted in the therapist, offer the mind of both a covenant in which they meet and join and are as one.

VII. The Ideal
Patient-Therapist Relationship

1. Who, then, is the therapist, and who is the patient? ²In the end, everyone is both. ³He who needs healing must heal. ⁴Physician, heal thyself. ⁵Who else is there to heal? ⁶And who else is in need of healing? ⁷Each patient who comes to a therapist offers him a chance to heal himself. ⁸He is therefore his therapist. ⁹And every therapist must learn to heal from each patient who comes to him. ¹⁰He thus becomes his patient. ¹¹God does not know of separation. ¹²What He knows is only that He has one Son. ¹³His

knowledge is reflected in the ideal patient-therapist relationship. [14]God comes to him who calls, and in Him he recognizes Himself.

2. Think carefully, teacher and therapist, for whom you pray, and who is in need of healing. [2]For therapy is prayer, and healing is its aim and its result. [3]What is prayer except the joining of minds in a relationship which Christ can enter? [4]This is His home, into which psychotherapy invites Him. [5]What is symptom cure, when another is always there to choose? [6]But once Christ enters in, what choice is there except to have Him stay? [7]There is no need for more than this, for it is everything. [8]Healing is here, and happiness and peace. [9]These are the "symptoms" of the ideal patient-therapist relationship, replacing those with which the patient came to ask for help.

3. The process that takes place in this relationship is actually one in which the therapist in his heart tells the patient that all his sins have been forgiven him, along with his own. [2]What could be the difference between healing and forgiveness? [3]Only Christ forgives, knowing His sinlessness. [4]His vision heals perception and sickness disappears. [5]Nor will it return again, once its cause has been removed. [6]This, however, needs the help of a very advanced thera-

pist, capable of joining with the patient in a holy relationship in which all sense of separation finally is overcome. 4. For this, one thing and one thing only is required: The therapist in no way confuses himself with God. ²All "unhealed healers" make this fundamental confusion in one form or another, because they must regard themselves as self-created rather than God-created. ³This confusion is rarely if ever in awareness, or the unhealed healer would instantly become a teacher of God, devoting his life to the function of true healing. ⁴Before he reached this point, he thought he was in charge of the therapeutic process and was therefore responsible for its outcome. ⁵His patient's errors thus became his own failures, and guilt became the cover, dark and strong, for what should be the Holiness of Christ. ⁶Guilt is inevitable in those who use their judgment in making their decisions. ⁷Guilt is impossible in those through whom the Holy Spirit speaks.

5. The passing of guilt is the true aim of therapy and the obvious aim of forgiveness. ²In this their oneness can be clearly seen. ³Yet who could experience the end of guilt who feels responsible for his brother in the role of guide for him? ⁴Such a function presupposes a knowledge that no one here can have; a certainty of past, present and fu-

ture, and of all the effects that may occur in them. [5]Only from this omniscient point of view would such a role be possible. [6]Yet no perception is omniscient, nor is the tiny self of one alone against the universe able to assume he has such wisdom except in madness. [7]That many therapists are mad is obvious. [8]No unhealed healer can be wholly sane.

6. Yet it is as insane not to accept a function God has given you as to invent one He has not. [2]The advanced therapist in no way can ever doubt the power that is in him. [3]Nor does he doubt its Source. [4]He understands all power in earth and Heaven belongs to him because of who he is. [5]And he is this because of his Creator, Whose Love is in him and Who cannot fail. [6]Think what this means; he has the gifts of God Himself to give away. [7]His patients are God's saints, who call upon his sanctity to make it theirs. [8]And as he gives it to them, they behold Christ's shining face as it looks back at them.

7. The insane, thinking they are God, are not afraid to offer weakness to God's Son. [2]But what they see in him because of this they fear indeed. [3]The unhealed healer cannot but be fearful of his patients, and suspect them of the treachery he sees in him. [4]He tries to heal, and thus at times he may. [5]But he will not succeed except to some extent and for a little while. [6]He does not see the Christ in

him who calls. [7]What answer can he give to one who seems to be a stranger; alien to the truth and poor in wisdom, without the god who must be given him? [8]Behold your God in him, for what you see will be your Answer.

8. Think what the joining of two brothers really means. [2]And then forget the world and all its little triumphs and its dreams of death. [3]The same are one, and nothing now can be remembered of the world of guilt. [4]The room becomes a temple, and the street a stream of stars that brushes lightly past all sickly dreams. [5]Healing is done, for what is perfect needs no healing, and what remains to be forgiven where there is no sin?

9. Be thankful, therapist, that you can see such things as this, if you but understand your proper role. [2]But if you fail in this, you have denied that God created you, and so you will not know you are His Son. [3]Who is your brother now? [4]What saint can come to take you home with him? [5]You lost the way. [6]And can you now expect to see in him an answer that you have refused to give? [7]Heal and be healed. [8]There is no other choice of pathways that can ever lead to peace. [9]O let your patient in, for he has come to you from God. [10]Is not his holiness enough to wake your memory of Him?

3

THE PRACTICE
OF PSYCHOTHERAPY

I. The Selection of Patients

1. Everyone who is sent to you is a patient of yours. [2]This does not mean that you select him, nor that you choose the kind of treatment that is suitable. [3]But it does mean that no one comes to you by mistake. [4]There are no errors in God's plan. [5]It would be an error, however, to assume that you know what to offer everyone who comes. [6]This is not up to you to decide. [7]There is a tendency to assume that you are being called on constantly to make sacrifices of yourself for those who come. [8]This could hardly be true. [9]To demand sacrifice of yourself is to demand a sacrifice of God, and He knows nothing of sacrifice. [10]Who could ask of Perfection that He be imperfect?

2. Who, then, decides what each brother needs? [2]Surely not you, who do not yet recognize who he is who asks.

³There is Something in him that will tell you, if you listen. ⁴And that is the answer; listen. ⁵Do not demand, do not decide, do not sacrifice. ⁶Listen. ⁷What you hear is true. ⁸Would God send His Son to you and not be sure you recognize his needs? ⁹Think what God is telling you; He needs your voice to speak for Him. ¹⁰Could anything be holier? ¹¹Or a greater gift to you? ¹²Would you rather choose who would be god, or hear the Voice of Him Who is God in you?

3. Your patients need not be physically present for you to serve them in the Name of God. ²This may be hard to remember, but God will not have His gifts to you limited to the few you actually see. ³You can see others as well, for seeing is not limited to the body's eyes. ⁴Some do not need your physical presence. ⁵They need you as much, and perhaps even more, at the instant they are sent. ⁶You will recognize them in whatever way can be most helpful to both of you. ⁷It does not matter how they come. ⁸They will be sent in whatever form is most helpful; a name, a thought, a picture, an idea, or perhaps just a feeling of reaching out to someone somewhere. ⁹The joining is in the hands of the Holy Spirit. ¹⁰It cannot fail to be accomplished.

4. A holy therapist, an advanced teacher of God, never forgets one thing; he did not make the curriculum of sal-

vation, nor did he establish his part in it. [2]He understands that his part is necessary to the whole, and that through it he will recognize the whole when his part is complete. [3]Meanwhile he must learn, and his patients are the means sent to him for his learning. [4]What could he be but grateful for them and to them? [5]They come bearing God. [6]Would he refuse this Gift for a pebble, or would he close the door on the savior of the world to let in a ghost? [7]Let him not betray the Son of God. [8]Who calls on him is far beyond his understanding. [9]Yet would he not rejoice that he can answer, when only thus will he be able to hear the call and understand that it is his?

II. Is Psychotherapy a Profession?

1. Strictly speaking the answer is no. [2]How could a separate profession be one in which everyone is engaged? [3]And how could any limits be laid on an interaction in which everyone is both patient and therapist in every relationship in which he enters? [4]Yet practically speaking, it can still be said that there are those who devote themselves primarily to healing of one sort or another as their

chief function. [5]And it is to them that a large number of others turn for help. [6]That, in effect, is the practice of therapy. [7]These are therefore "officially" helpers. [8]They are devoted to certain kinds of needs in their professional activities, although they may be far more able teachers outside of them. [9]These people need no special rules, of course, but they may be called upon to use special applications of the general principles of healing.

2. First, the professional therapist is in an excellent position to demonstrate that there is no order of difficulty in healing. [2]For this, however, he needs special training, because the curriculum by which he became a therapist probably taught him little or nothing about the real principles of healing. [3]In fact, it probably taught him how to make healing impossible. [4]Most of the world's teaching follows a curriculum in judgment, with the aim of making the therapist a judge.

3. Even this the Holy Spirit can use, and will use, given the slightest invitation. [2]The unhealed healer may be arrogant, selfish, unconcerned, and actually dishonest. [3]He may be uninterested in healing as his major goal. [4]Yet something happened to him, however slight it may have been, when he chose to be a healer, however misguided the direction he may have chosen. [5]That "something" is

enough. ⁶Sooner or later that something will rise and grow; a patient will touch his heart, and the therapist will silently ask him for help. ⁷He has himself found a therapist. ⁸He has asked the Holy Spirit to enter the relationship and heal it. ⁹He has accepted the Atonement for himself.

4. God is said to have looked on all He created and pronounced it good. ²No, He declared it perfect, and so it was. ³And since His creations do not change and last forever, so it is now. ⁴Yet neither a perfect therapist nor a perfect patient can possibly exist. ⁵Both must have denied their perfection, for their very need for each other implies a sense of lack. ⁶A one-to-one relationship is not One Relationship. ⁷Yet it is the means of return; the way God chose for the return of His Son. ⁸In that strange dream a strange correction must enter, for only that is the call to awake. ⁹And what else should therapy be? ¹⁰Awake and be glad, for all your sins have been forgiven you. ¹¹This is the only message that any two should ever give each other.

5. Something good must come from every meeting of patient and therapist. ²And that good is saved for both, against the day when they can recognize that only that was real in their relationship. ³At that moment the good is returned to them, blessed by the Holy Spirit as a gift from

their Creator as a sign of His Love. ⁴For the therapeutic relationship must become like the relationship of the Father and the Son. ⁵There is no other, for there is nothing else. ⁶The therapists of this world do not expect this outcome, and many of their patients would not be able to accept help from them if they did. ⁷Yet no therapist really sets the goal for the relationships of which he is a part. ⁸His understanding begins with recognizing this, and then goes on from there.

6. It is in the instant that the therapist forgets to judge the patient that healing occurs. ²In some relationships this point is never reached, although both patient and therapist may change their dreams in the process. ³Yet it will not be the same dream for both of them, and so it is not the dream of forgiveness in which both will someday wake. ⁴The good is saved; indeed is cherished. ⁵But only little time is saved. ⁶The new dreams will lose their temporary appeal and turn to dreams of fear, which is the content of all dreams. ⁷Yet no patient can accept more than he is ready to receive, and no therapist can offer more than he believes he has. ⁸And so there is a place for all relationships in this world, and they will bring as much good as each can accept and use.

7. Yet it is when judgment ceases that healing occurs, because only then it can be understood that there is no order of difficulty in healing. [2]This is a necessary understanding for the healed healer. [3]He has learned that it is no harder to wake a brother from one dream than from another. [4]No professional therapist can hold this understanding consistently in his mind, offering it to all who come to him. [5]There are some in this world who have come very close, but they have not accepted the gift entirely in order to stay and let their understanding remain on earth until the closing of time. [6]They could hardly be called professional therapists. [7]They are the Saints of God. [8]They are the Saviors of the world. [9]Their image remains, because they have chosen that it be so. [10]They take the place of other images, and help with kindly dreams.

8. Once the professional therapist has realized that minds are joined, he can also recognize that order of difficulty in healing is meaningless. [2]Yet well before he reaches this in time he can go towards it. [3]Many holy instants can be his along the way. [4]A goal marks the end of a journey, not the beginning, and as each goal is reached another can be dimly seen ahead. [5]Most professional therapists are still at the very start of the beginning stage of the first journey.

[6]Even those who have begun to understand what they must do may still oppose the setting-out. [7]Yet all the laws of healing can be theirs in just an instant. [8]The journey is not long except in dreams.

9. The professional therapist has one advantage that can save enormous time if it is properly used. [2]He has chosen a road in which there is great temptation to misuse his role. [3]This enables him to pass by many obstacles to peace quite quickly, if he escapes the temptation to assume a function that has not been given him. [4]To understand there is no order of difficulty in healing, he must also recognize the equality of himself and the patient. [5]There is no halfway point in this. [6]Either they are equal or not. [7]The attempts of therapists to compromise in this respect are strange indeed. [8]Some utilize the relationship merely to collect bodies to worship at their shrine, and this they regard as healing. [9]Many patients, too, consider this strange procedure as salvation. [10]Yet at each meeting there is One Who says, "My brother, choose again."

10. Do not forget that any form of specialness must be defended, and will be. [2]The defenseless therapist has the strength of God with him, but the defensive therapist has lost sight of the Source of his salvation. [3]He does not see

and he does not hear. [4]How, then, can he teach? [5]Because it is the Will of God that he take his place in the plan for salvation. [6]Because it is the Will of God that his patient be helped to join with him there. [7]Because his inability to see and hear does not limit the Holy Spirit in any way. [8]Except in time. [9]In time there can be a great lag between the offering and the acceptance of healing. [10]This is the veil across the face of Christ. [11]Yet it can be but an illusion, because time does not exist and the Will of God has always been exactly as it is.

III. The Question of Payment

1. No one can pay for therapy, for healing is of God and He asks for nothing. [2]It is, however, part of His plan that everything in this world be used by the Holy Spirit to help in carrying out the plan. [3]Even an advanced therapist has some earthly needs while he is here. [4]Should he need money it will be given him, not in payment, but to help him better serve the plan. [5]Money is not evil. [6]It is nothing. [7]But no one here can live with no illusions, for he must yet strive to have the last illusion be accepted by

everyone everywhere. [8]He has a mighty part in this one purpose, for which he came. [9]He stays here but for this. [10]And while he stays he will be given what he needs to stay.

2. Only an unhealed healer would try to heal for money, and he will not succeed to the extent to which he values it. [2]Nor will he find his healing in the process. [3]There will be those of whom the Holy Spirit asks some payment for His purpose. [4]There will be those from whom He does not ask. [5]It should not be the therapist who makes these decisions. [6]There is a difference between payment and cost. [7]To give money where God's plan allots it has no cost. [8]To withhold it from where it rightfully belongs has enormous cost. [9]The therapist who would do this loses the name of healer, for he could never understand what healing is. [10]He cannot give it, and so he does not have it.

3. The therapists of this world are indeed useless to the world's salvation. [2]They make demands, and so they cannot give. [3]Patients can pay only for the exchange of illusions. [4]This, indeed, must demand payment, and the cost is great. [5]A "bought" relationship cannot offer the only gift whereby all healing is accomplished. [6]Forgiveness, the Holy Spirit's only dream, must have no cost. [7]For if it does, it merely crucifies God's Son again. [8]Can this be

how he is forgiven? ⁹Can this be how the dream of sin will end?

4. The right to live is something no one need fight for. ²It is promised him, and guaranteed by God. ³Therefore it is a right the therapist and patient share alike. ⁴If their relationship is to be holy, whatever one needs is given by the other; whatever one lacks the other supplies. ⁵Herein is the relationship made holy, for herein both are healed. ⁶The therapist repays the patient in gratitude, as does the patient repay him. ⁷There is no cost to either. ⁸But thanks are due to both, for the release from long imprisonment and doubt. ⁹Who would not be grateful for such a gift? ¹⁰Yet who could possibly imagine that it could be bought?

5. It has well been said that to him who hath shall be given. ²Because he has, he can give. ³And because he gives, he shall be given. ⁴This is the law of God, and not of the world. ⁵So it is with God's healers. ⁶They give because they have heard His Word and understood it. ⁷All that they need will thus be given them. ⁸But they will lose this understanding unless they remember that all they have comes only from God. ⁹If they believe they need anything from a brother, they will recognize him as a brother no longer. ¹⁰And if they do this, a light goes out even in Heaven. ¹¹Where God's Son turns against himself, he can

look only upon darkness. [12]He has himself denied the light, and cannot see.

6. One rule should always be observed: No one should be turned away because he cannot pay. [2]No one is sent by accident to anyone. [3]Relationships are always purposeful. [4]Whatever their purpose may have been before the Holy Spirit entered them, they are always His potential temple; the resting place of Christ and home of God Himself. [5]Whoever comes has been sent. [6]Perhaps he was sent to give his brother the money he needed. [7]Both will be blessed thereby. [8]Perhaps he was sent to teach the therapist how much he needs forgiveness, and how valueless is money in comparison. [9]Again will both be blessed. [10]Only in terms of cost could one have more. [11]In sharing, everyone must gain a blessing without cost.

7. This view of payment may well seem impractical, and in the eyes of the world it would be so. [2]Yet not one worldly thought is really practical. [3]How much is gained by striving for illusions? [4]How much is lost by throwing God away? [5]And is it possible to do so? [6]Surely it is impractical to strive for nothing, and to attempt to do what is impossible. [7]Then stop a while, long enough to think of this: You have perhaps been seeking for salvation without recognizing where to look. [8]Whoever asks your help can

show you where. ⁹What greater gift than this could you be given? ¹⁰What greater gift is there that you would give?

8. Physician, healer, therapist, teacher, heal thyself. ²Many will come to you carrying the gift of healing, if you so elect. ³The Holy Spirit never refuses an invitation to enter and abide with you. ⁴He will give you endless opportunities to open the door to your salvation, for such is His function. ⁵He will also tell you exactly what your function is in every circumstance and at all times. ⁶Whoever He sends you will reach you, holding out his hand to his Friend. ⁷Let the Christ in you bid him welcome, for that same Christ is in him as well. ⁸Deny him entrance, and you have denied the Christ in you. ⁹Remember the sorrowful story of the world, and the glad tidings of salvation. ¹⁰Remember the plan of God for the restoration of joy and peace. ¹¹And do not forget how very simple are the ways of God:

¹²You were lost in the darkness of the world until you asked for light. ¹³And then God sent His Son to give it to you.

THE SONG OF PRAYER

Prayer, Forgiveness, Healing

An Extension of the Principles of

A Course in Miracles

SECOND EDITION

CONTENTS

THE SONG
OF PRAYER

Prayer, Forgiveness, Healing

1

PRAYER

Introduction

1. Prayer is the greatest gift with which God blessed His Son at his creation. [2]It was then what it is to become; the single voice Creator and creation share; the song the Son sings to the Father, Who returns the thanks it offers Him unto the Son. [3]Endless the harmony, and endless, too, the joyous concord of the Love They give forever to Each Other. [4]And in this, creation is extended. [5]God gives thanks to His extension in His Son. [6]His Son gives thanks for his creation, in the song of his creating in his Father's Name. [7]The Love They share is what all prayer will be throughout eternity, when time is done. [8]For such it was before time seemed to be.

2. To you who are in time a little while, prayer takes the form that best will suit your need. [2]You have but one.

³What God created one must recognize its oneness, and rejoice that what illusions seemed to separate is one forever in the Mind of God. ⁴Prayer now must be the means by which God's Son leaves separate goals and separate interests by, and turns in holy gladness to the truth of union in his Father and himself.

3. Lay down your dreams, you holy Son of God, and rising up as God created you, dispense with idols and remember Him. ²Prayer will sustain you now, and bless you as you lift your heart to Him in rising song that reaches higher and then higher still, until both high and low have disappeared. ³Faith in your goal will grow and hold you up as you ascend the shining stairway to the lawns of Heaven and the gate of peace. ⁴For this is prayer, and here salvation is. ⁵This is the way. ⁶It is God's gift to you.

I. True Prayer

1. Prayer is a way offered by the Holy Spirit to reach God. ²It is not merely a question or an entreaty. ³It cannot succeed until you realize that it asks for nothing. ⁴How else could it serve its purpose? ⁵It is impossible to pray for idols and hope to reach God. ⁶True prayer must avoid the

pitfall of asking to entreat. ⁷Ask, rather, to receive what is already given; to accept what is already there.

2. You have been told to ask the Holy Spirit for the answer to any specific problem, and that you will receive a specific answer if such is your need. ²You have also been told that there is only one problem and one answer. ³In prayer this is not contradictory. ⁴There are decisions to make here, and they must be made whether they be illusions or not. ⁵You cannot be asked to accept answers which are beyond the level of need that you can recognize. ⁶Therefore, it is not the form of the question that matters, nor how it is asked. ⁷The form of the answer, if given by God, will suit your need as you see it. ⁸This is merely an echo of the reply of His Voice. ⁹The real sound is always a song of thanksgiving and of Love.

3. You cannot, then, ask for the echo. ²It is the song that is the gift. ³Along with it come the overtones, the harmonics, the echoes, but these are secondary. ⁴In true prayer you hear only the song. ⁵All the rest is merely added. ⁶You have sought first the Kingdom of Heaven, and all else has indeed been given you.

4. The secret of true prayer is to forget the things you think you need. ²To ask for the specific is much the same as to look on sin and then forgive it. ³Also in the same

way, in prayer you overlook your specific needs as you see them, and let them go into God's Hands. ⁴There they become your gifts to Him, for they tell Him that you would have no gods before Him; no Love but His. ⁵What could His answer be but your remembrance of Him? ⁶Can this be traded for a bit of trifling advice about a problem of an instant's duration? ⁷God answers only for eternity. ⁸But still all little answers are contained in this.

5. Prayer is a stepping aside; a letting go, a quiet time of listening and loving. ²It should not be confused with supplication of any kind, because it is a way of remembering your holiness. ³Why should holiness entreat, being fully entitled to everything Love has to offer? ⁴And it is to Love you go in prayer. ⁵Prayer is an offering; a giving up of yourself to be at one with Love. ⁶There is nothing to ask because there is nothing left to want. ⁷That nothingness becomes the altar of God. ⁸It disappears in Him.

6. This is not a level of prayer that everyone can attain as yet. ²Those who have not reached it still need your help in prayer because their asking is not yet based upon acceptance. ³Help in prayer does not mean that another mediates between you and God. ⁴But it does mean that another stands beside you and helps to raise you up to Him. ⁵One who has realized the goodness of God prays without fear.

⁶And one who prays without fear cannot but reach Him. ⁷He can therefore also reach His Son, wherever he may be and whatever form he may seem to take.

7. Praying to Christ in anyone is true prayer because it is a gift of thanks to His Father. ²To ask that Christ be but Himself is not an entreaty. ³It is a song of thanksgiving for what you are. ⁴Herein lies the power of prayer. ⁵It asks nothing and receives everything. ⁶This prayer can be shared because it receives for everyone. ⁷To pray with one who knows that this is true is to be answered. ⁸Perhaps the specific form of resolution for a specific problem will occur to either of you; it does not matter which. ⁹Perhaps it will reach both, if you are genuinely attuned to one another. ¹⁰It will come because you have realized that Christ is in both of you. ¹¹That is its only truth.

II. The Ladder of Prayer

1. Prayer has no beginning and no end. ²It is a part of life. ³But it does change in form, and grow with learning until it reaches its formless state, and fuses into total communication with God. ⁴In its asking form it need not, and often does not, make appeal to God, or even involve belief in

Him. ⁵At these levels prayer is merely wanting, out of a sense of scarcity and lack.

2. These forms of prayer, or asking-out-of-need, always involve feelings of weakness and inadequacy, and could never be made by a Son of God who knows Who he is. ²No one, then, who is sure of his Identity could pray in these forms. ³Yet it is also true that no one who is uncertain of his Identity can avoid praying in this way. ⁴And prayer is as continual as life. ⁵Everyone prays without ceasing. ⁶Ask and you have received, for you have established what it is you want.

3. It is also possible to reach a higher form of asking-out-of-need, for in this world prayer is reparative, and so it must entail levels of learning. ²Here, the asking may be addressed to God in honest belief, though not yet with understanding. ³A vague and usually unstable sense of identification has generally been reached, but tends to be blurred by a deep-rooted sense of sin. ⁴It is possible at this level to continue to ask for things of this world in various forms, and it is also possible to ask for gifts such as honesty or goodness, and particularly for forgiveness for the many sources of guilt that inevitably underlie any prayer of need. ⁵Without guilt there is no scarcity. ⁶The sinless have no needs.

4. At this level also comes that curious contradiction in terms known as "praying for one's enemies." ²The contradiction lies not in the actual words, but rather in the way in which they are usually interpreted. ³While you believe you have enemies, you have limited prayer to the laws of this world, and have also limited your ability to receive and to accept to the same narrow margins. ⁴And yet, if you have enemies you have need of prayer, and great need, too. ⁵What does the phrase really mean? ⁶Pray for yourself, that you may not seek to imprison Christ and thereby lose the recognition of your own Identity. ⁷Be traitor to no one, or you will be treacherous to yourself.

5. An enemy is the symbol of an imprisoned Christ. ²And who could He be except yourself? ³The prayer for enemies thus becomes a prayer for your own freedom. ⁴Now it is no longer a contradiction in terms. ⁵It has become a statement of the unity of Christ and a recognition of His sinlessness. ⁶And now it has become holy, for it acknowledges the Son of God as he was created.

6. Let it never be forgotten that prayer at any level is always for yourself. ²If you unite with anyone in prayer, you make him part of you. ³The enemy is you, as is the Christ. ⁴Before it can become holy, then, prayer becomes a choice. ⁵You do not choose for another. ⁶You can but choose for

yourself. [7]Pray truly for your enemies, for herein lies your own salvation. [8]Forgive them for your sins, and you will be forgiven indeed.

7. Prayer is a ladder reaching up to Heaven. [2]At the top there is a transformation much like your own, for prayer is part of you. [3]The things of earth are left behind, all unremembered. [4]There is no asking, for there is no lack. [5]Identity in Christ is fully recognized as set forever, beyond all change and incorruptible. [6]The light no longer flickers, and will never go out. [7]Now, without needs of any kind, and clad forever in the pure sinlessness that is the gift of God to you, His Son, prayer can again become what it was meant to be. [8]For now it rises as a song of thanks to your Creator, sung without words, or thoughts, or vain desires, unneedful now of anything at all. [9]So it extends, as it was meant to do. [10]And for this giving God Himself gives thanks.

8. God is the goal of every prayer, giving it timelessness instead of end. [2]Nor has it a beginning, because the goal has never changed. [3]Prayer in its earlier forms is an illusion, because there is no need for a ladder to reach what one has never left. [4]Yet prayer is part of forgiveness as long as forgiveness, itself an illusion, remains unattained. [5]Prayer is tied up with learning until the goal of learning has been

reached. ⁶And then all things will be transformed together, and returned unblemished into the Mind of God. ⁷Being beyond learning, this state cannot be described. ⁸The stages necessary to its attainment, however, need to be understood, if peace is to be restored to God's Son, who lives now with the illusion of death and the fear of God.

III. Praying for Others

1. We said that prayer is always for yourself, and this is so. ²Why, then, should you pray for others at all? ³And if you should, how should you do it? ⁴Praying for others, if rightly understood, becomes a means for lifting your projections of guilt from your brother, and enabling you to recognize it is not he who is hurting you. ⁵The poisonous thought that he *is* your enemy, your evil counterpart, your nemesis, must be relinquished before *you* can be saved from guilt. ⁶For this the means is prayer, of rising power and with ascending goals, until it reaches even up to God.

2. The earlier forms of prayer, at the bottom of the ladder, will not be free from envy and malice. ²They call for vengeance, not for love. ³Nor do they come from one who understands that they are calls for death, made out of fear by

those who cherish guilt. ⁴They call upon a vengeful god, and it is he who seems to answer them. ⁵Hell cannot be asked for another, and then escaped by him who asks for it. ⁶Only those who are in hell can ask for hell. ⁷Those who have been forgiven, and who accepted their forgiveness, could never make a prayer like that.

3. At these levels, then, the learning goal must be to recognize that prayer will bring an answer only in the form in which the prayer was made. ²This is enough. ³From here it will be an easy step to the next levels. ⁴The next ascent begins with this:

⁵What I have asked for for my brother is not what I would have. ⁶Thus have I made of him my enemy.

⁷It is apparent that this step cannot be reached by anyone who sees no value or advantage to himself in setting others free. ⁸This may be long delayed, because it may seem to be dangerous instead of merciful. ⁹To the guilty there seems indeed to be a real advantage in having enemies, and this imagined gain must go, if enemies are to be set free.

4. Guilt must be given up, and not concealed. ²Nor can

this be done without some pain, and a glimpse of the merciful nature of this step may for some time be followed by a deep retreat into fear. ³For fear's defenses are fearful in themselves, and when they are recognized they bring their fear with them. ⁴Yet what advantage has an illusion of escape ever brought a prisoner? ⁵His real escape from guilt can lie only in the recognition that the guilt has gone. ⁶And how can this be recognized as long as he hides it in another, and does not see it as his own? ⁷Fear of escape makes it difficult to welcome freedom, and to make a jailer of an enemy seems to be safety. ⁸How, then, can he be released without an insane fear for yourself? ⁹You have made of him your salvation and your escape from guilt. ¹⁰Your investment in this escape is heavy, and your fear of letting it go is strong.

5. Stand still an instant, now, and think what you have done. ²Do not forget that it is you who did it, and who can therefore let it go. ³Hold out your hand. ⁴This enemy has come to bless you. ⁵Take his blessing, and feel how your heart is lifted and your fear released. ⁶Do not hold on to it, nor onto him. ⁷He is a Son of God, along with you. ⁸He is no jailer, but a messenger of Christ. ⁹Be this to him, that you may see him thus.

6. It is not easy to realize that prayers for things, for status, for human love, for external "gifts" of any kind, are always made to set up jailers and to hide from guilt. ²These things are used for goals that substitute for God, and therefore distort the purpose of prayer. ³The desire for them *is* the prayer. ⁴One need not ask explicitly. ⁵The goal of God is lost in the quest for lesser goals of any kind, and prayer becomes requests for enemies. ⁶The power of prayer can be quite clearly recognized even in this. ⁷No one who wants an enemy will fail to find one. ⁸But just as surely will he lose the only true goal that is given him. ⁹Think of the cost, and understand it well. ¹⁰All other ygoals are at the cost of God.

IV. Praying with Others

1. Until the second level at least begins, one cannot share in prayer. ²For until that point, each one must ask for different things. ³But once the need to hold the other as an enemy has been questioned, and the reason for doing so has been recognized if only for an instant, it becomes possible to join in prayer. ⁴Enemies do not share a goal. ⁵It is in this their enmity is kept. ⁶Their separate wishes are

their arsenals; their fortresses in hate. ⁷The key to rising further still in prayer lies in this simple thought; this change of mind:

⁸We go together, you and I.

2. Now it is possible to help in prayer, and so reach up yourself. ²This step begins the quicker ascent, but there are still many lessons to learn. ³The way is open, and hope is justified. ⁴Yet it is likely at first that what is asked for even by those who join in prayer is not the goal that prayer should truly seek. ⁵Even together you may ask for things, and thus set up but an illusion of a goal you share. ⁶You may ask together for specifics, and not realize that you are asking for effects without the cause. ⁷And this you cannot have. ⁸For no one can receive effects alone, asking a cause from which they do not come to offer them to him.

3. Even the joining, then, is not enough, if those who pray together do not ask, before all else, what is the Will of God. ²From this Cause only can the answer come in which are all specifics satisfied; all separate wishes unified in one. ³Prayer for specifics always asks to have the past repeated in some way. ⁴What was enjoyed before, or

seemed to be; what was another's and he seemed to love,—all these are but illusions from the past. ⁵The aim of prayer is to release the present from its chains of past illusions; to let it be a freely chosen remedy from every choice that stood for a mistake. ⁶What prayer can offer now so far exceeds all that you asked before that it is pitiful to be content with less.

4. You have chosen a newborn chance each time you pray. ²And would you stifle and imprison it in ancient prisons, when the chance has come to free yourself from all of them at once? ³Do not restrict your asking. ⁴Prayer can bring the peace of God. ⁵What time-bound thing can give you more than this, in just the little space that lasts until it crumbles into dust?

V. The Ladder Ends

1. Prayer is a way to true humility. ²And here again it rises slowly up, and grows in strength and love and holiness. ³Let it but leave the ground where it begins to rise to God, and true humility will come at last to grace the mind that thought it was alone and stood against the world. ⁴Humil-

ity brings peace because it does not claim that you must rule the universe, nor judge all things as you would have them be. ⁵All little gods it gladly lays aside, not in resentment, but in honesty and recognition that they do not serve.

2. Illusions and humility have goals so far apart they cannot coexist, nor share a dwelling place where they can meet. ²Where one has come the other disappears. ³The truly humble have no goal but God because they need no idols, and defense no longer serves a purpose. ⁴Enemies are useless now, because humility does not oppose. ⁵It does not hide in shame because it is content with what it is, knowing creation is the Will of God. ⁶Its selflessness is Self, and this it sees in every meeting, where it gladly joins with every Son of God, whose purity it recognizes that it shares with him.

3. Now prayer is lifted from the world of things, of bodies, and of gods of every kind, and you can rest in holiness at last. ²Humility has come to teach you how to understand your glory as God's Son, and recognize the arrogance of sin. ³A dream has veiled the face of Christ from you. ⁴Now can you look upon His sinlessness. ⁵High has the ladder risen. ⁶You have come almost to Heaven.

⁷There is little more to learn before the journey is complete. ⁸Now can you say to everyone who comes to join in prayer with you:

⁹I cannot go without you, for you are a part of me.

¹⁰And so he is in truth. ¹¹Now can you pray only for what you truly share with him. ¹²For you have understood he never left, and you, who seemed alone, are one with him. 4. The ladder ends with this, for learning is no longer needed. ²Now you stand before the gate of Heaven, and your brother stands beside you there. ³The lawns are deep and still, for here the place appointed for the time when you should come has waited long for you. ⁴Here will time end forever. ⁵At this gate eternity itself will join with you. ⁶Prayer has become what it was meant to be, for you have recognized the Christ in you.

2

FORGIVENESS

Introduction

1. Forgiveness offers wings to prayer, to make its rising easy and its progress swift. ²Without its strong support it would be vain to try to rise above prayer's bottom step, or even to attempt to climb at all. ³Forgiveness is prayer's ally; sister in the plan for your salvation. ⁴Both must come to hold you up and keep your feet secure; your purpose steadfast and unchangeable. ⁵Behold the greatest help that God ordained to be with you until you reach to Him. ⁶Illusion's end will come with this. ⁷Unlike the timeless nature of its sister, prayer, forgiveness has an end. ⁸For it becomes unneeded when the rising up is done. ⁹Yet now it has a purpose beyond which you cannot go, nor have you need to go. ¹⁰Accomplish this and you have been re-

deemed. [11]Accomplish this and you have been trans-formed. [12]Accomplish this and you will save the world.

I. Forgiveness of Yourself

1. No gift of Heaven has been more misunderstood than has forgiveness. [2]It has, in fact, become a scourge; a curse where it was meant to bless, a cruel mockery of grace, a parody upon the holy peace of God. [3]Yet those who have not yet chosen to begin the steps of prayer cannot but use it thus. [4]Forgiveness' kindness is obscure at first, because salvation is not understood, *nor truly sought for.* [5]What was meant to heal is used to hurt because forgiveness is not wanted. [6]Guilt becomes salvation, and the remedy appears to be a terrible alternative to life.

2. Forgiveness-to-destroy will therefore suit the purpose of the world far better than its true objective, and the honest means by which this goal is reached. [2]Forgiveness-to-destroy will overlook no sin, no crime, no guilt that it can seek and find and "love." [3]Dear to its heart is error, and mistakes loom large and grow and swell within its sight. [4]It carefully picks out all evil things, and overlooks the loving as a plague; a hateful thing of danger and of death.

⁵Forgiveness-to-destroy *is* death, and this it sees in all it looks upon and hates. ⁶God's mercy has become a twisted knife that would destroy the holy Son He loves.

3. Would you forgive yourself for doing this? ²Then learn that God has given you the means by which you can return to Him in peace. ³*Do not see error.* ⁴Do not make it real. ⁵Select the loving and forgive the sin by choosing in its place the face of Christ. ⁶How otherwise can prayer return to God? ⁷He loves His Son. ⁸Can you remember Him and hate what He created? ⁹You will hate his Father if you hate the Son He loves. ¹⁰For as you see the Son you see yourself, and as you see yourself is God to you.

4. As prayer is always for yourself, so is forgiveness always given you. ²It is impossible to forgive another, for it is only your sins you see in him. ³You want to see them there, and not in you. ⁴That is why forgiveness of another is an illusion. ⁵Yet it is the only happy dream in all the world; the only one that does not lead to death. ⁶Only in someone else can you forgive yourself, for you have called him guilty of your sins, and in him must your innocence now be found. ⁷Who but the sinful need to be forgiven? ⁸And do not ever think you can see sin in anyone except yourself.

5. This is the great deception of the world, and you the

great deceiver of yourself. ²It always seems to be another who is evil, and in his sin you are the injured one. ³How could freedom be possible if this were so? ⁴You would be slave to everyone, for what he does entails your fate, your feelings, your despair or hope, your misery or joy. ⁵You have no freedom unless he gives it to you. ⁶And being evil, he can only give of what he is. ⁷You cannot see his sins and not your own. ⁸But you can free him and yourself as well.

6. Forgiveness, truly given, is the way in which your only hope of freedom lies. ²Others will make mistakes and so will you, as long as this illusion of a world appears to be your home. ³Yet God Himself has given all His Sons a remedy for all illusions that they think they see. ⁴Christ's vision does not use your eyes, but you can look through His and learn to see like Him. ⁵Mistakes are tiny shadows, quickly gone, that for an instant only seem to hide the face of Christ, which still remains unchanged behind them all. ⁶His constancy remains in tranquil silence and in perfect peace. ⁷He does not know of shadows. ⁸His the eyes that look past error to the Christ in you.

7. Ask, then, His help, and ask Him how to learn forgiveness as His vision lets it be. ²You are in need of what He gives, and your salvation rests on learning this of Him.

³Prayer cannot be released to Heaven while forgiveness-to-destroy remains with you. ⁴God's mercy would remove this withering and poisoned thinking from your holy mind. ⁵Christ has forgiven you, and in His sight the world becomes as holy as Himself. ⁶Who sees no evil in it sees like Him. ⁷For what He has forgiven has not sinned, and guilt can be no more. ⁸Salvation's plan is made complete, and sanity has come.

8. Forgiveness is the call to sanity, for who but the insane would look on sin when he could see the face of Christ instead? ²This is the choice you can make; the simplest one, and yet the only one that you *can* make. ³God calls on you to save His Son from death by offering Christ's Love to him. ⁴This is your need, and God holds out this gift to you. ⁵As He would give, so must you give as well. ⁶And thus is prayer restored to formlessness, beyond all limits into timelessness, with nothing of the past to hold it back from re-uniting with the ceaseless song that all creation sings unto its God.

9. But to achieve this end you first must learn, before you reach where learning cannot go. ²Forgiveness is the key, but who can use a key when he has lost the door for which the key was made, and where alone it fits? ³Therefore we make distinctions, so that prayer can be released

from darkness into light. ⁴Forgiveness' role must be reversed, and cleansed from evil usages and hateful goals. ⁵Forgiveness-to-destroy must be unveiled in all its treachery, and then let go forever and forever. ⁶There can be no trace of it remaining, if the plan that God established for returning be achieved at last, and learning be complete.

10. This is the world of opposites. ²And you must choose between them every instant while this world retains reality for you. ³Yet you must learn alternatives for choice, or you will not be able to attain your freedom. ⁴Let it then be clear to you exactly what forgiveness means to you, and learn what it should be to set you free. ⁵The level of your prayer depends on this, for here it waits its freedom to ascend above the world of chaos into peace.

II. Forgiveness-to-Destroy

1. Forgiveness-to-destroy has many forms, being a weapon of the world of form. ²Not all of them are obvious, and some are carefully concealed beneath what seems like charity. ³Yet all the forms that it may seem to take have but this single goal; their purpose is to separate and make what God created equal, different. ⁴The difference is clear

in several forms where the designed comparison cannot be missed, nor is it really meant to be.

2. In this group, first, there are the forms in which a "better" person deigns to stoop to save a "baser" one from what he truly is. ²Forgiveness here rests on an attitude of gracious lordliness so far from love that arrogance could never be dislodged. ³Who can forgive and yet despise? ⁴And who can tell another he is steeped in sin, and yet perceive him as the Son of God? ⁵Who makes a slave to teach what freedom is? ⁶There is no union here, but only grief. ⁷This is not really mercy. ⁸This is death.

3. Another form, still very like the first if it is understood, does not appear in quite such blatant arrogance. ²The one who would forgive the other does not claim to be the better. ³Now he says instead that here is one whose sinfulness he shares, since both have been unworthy and deserve the retribution of the wrath of God. ⁴This can appear to be a humble thought, and may indeed induce a rivalry in sinfulness and guilt. ⁵It is not love for God's creation and the holiness that is His gift forever. ⁶Can His Son condemn himself and still remember Him?

4. Here the goal is to separate from God the Son He loves, and keep him from his Source. ²This goal is also sought by those who seek the role of martyr at another's hand.

³Here must the aim be clearly seen, for this may pass as meekness and as charity instead of cruelty. ⁴Is it not kind to be accepting of another's spite, and not respond except with silence and a gentle smile? ⁵Behold, how good are you who bear with patience and with saintliness the anger and the hurt another gives, and do not show the bitter pain you feel.

5. Forgiveness-to-destroy will often hide behind a cloak like this. ²It shows the face of suffering and pain, in silent proof of guilt and of the ravages of sin. ³Such is the witness that it offers one who could be savior, not an enemy. ⁴But having been made enemy, he must accept the guilt and heavy-laid reproach that thus is put upon him. ⁵Is this love? ⁶Or is it rather treachery to one who needs salvation from the pain of guilt? ⁷What could the purpose be, except to keep the witnesses of guilt away from love?

6. Forgiveness-to-destroy can also take the form of bargaining and compromise. ²"I will forgive you if you meet my needs, for in your slavery is my release." ³Say this to anyone and you are slave. ⁴And you will seek to rid yourself of guilt in further bargains which can give no hope, but only greater pain and misery. ⁵How fearful has forgiveness now become, and how distorted is the end it

seeks. ⁶Have mercy on yourself who bargains thus. ⁷God gives and does not ask for recompense. ⁸There is no giving but to give like Him. ⁹All else is mockery. ¹⁰For who would try to strike a bargain with the Son of God, and thank his Father for his holiness?

7. What would you show your brother? ²Would you try to reinforce his guilt and thus your own? ³Forgiveness is the means for your escape. ⁴How pitiful it is to make of it the means for further slavery and pain. ⁵Within the world of opposites there is a way to use forgiveness for the goal of God, and find the peace He offers you. ⁶Take nothing else, or you have sought your death, and prayed for separation from your Self. ⁷Christ is for all because He is in all. ⁸It is His face forgiveness lets you see. ⁹It is His face in which you see your own.

8. All forms forgiveness takes that do not lead away from anger, condemnation and comparisons of every kind are death. ²For that is what their purposes have set. ³Be not deceived by them, but lay them by as worthless in their tragic offerings. ⁴You do not want to stay in slavery. ⁵You do not want to be afraid of God. ⁶You want to see the sunlight and the glow of Heaven shining on the face of earth, redeemed from sin and in the Love of God. ⁷From here is

prayer released, along with you. ⁸Your wings are free, and prayer will lift you up and bring you home where God would have you be.

III. Forgiveness-for-Salvation

1. Forgiveness-for-salvation has one form, and only one. ²It does not ask for proof of innocence, nor pay of any kind. ³It does not argue, nor evaluate the errors that it wants to overlook. ⁴It does not offer gifts in treachery, nor promise freedom while it asks for death. ⁵Would God deceive you? ⁶He but asks for trust and willingness to learn how to be free. ⁷He gives His Teacher to whoever asks, and seeks to understand the Will of God. ⁸His readiness to give lies far beyond your understanding and your simple grasp. ⁹Yet He has willed you learn the way to Him, and in His willing there is certainty.

2. You child of God, the gifts of God are yours, not by your plans but by His holy Will. ²His Voice will teach you what forgiveness is, and how to give it as He wills it be. ³Do not, then, seek to understand what is beyond you yet, but let it be a way to draw you up to where the eyes of Christ become the sight you choose. ⁴Give up all else, for

there *is* nothing else. ⁵When someone calls for help in any form, He is the One to answer for you. ⁶All that you need do is to step back and not to interfere. ⁷Forgiveness-for-salvation is His task, and it is He Who will respond for you.

3. Do not establish what the form should be that Christ's forgiveness takes. ²He knows the way to make of every call a help to you, as you arise in haste to go at last unto your Father's house. ³Now can He make your footsteps sure, your words sincere; not with your own sincerity, but with His Own. ⁴Let Him take charge of how you would forgive, and each occasion then will be to you another step to Heaven and to peace.

4. Are you not weary of imprisonment? ²God did not choose this sorry path for you. ³What you have chosen still can be undone, for prayer is merciful and God is just. ⁴His is a justice He can understand, but you cannot as yet. ⁵Still will He give the means to you to learn of Him, and know at last that condemnation is not real and makes illusions in its evil name. ⁶And yet it matters not the form that dreams may seem to take. ⁷Illusions are untrue. ⁸God's Will is truth, and you are one with Him in Will and purpose. ⁹Here all dreams are done.

5. "What should I do for him, Your holy Son?" should be

the only thing you ever ask when help is needed and for-giveness sought. ²The form the seeking takes you need not judge. ³And let it not be you who sets the form in which forgiveness comes to save God's Son. ⁴The light of Christ in him is his release, and it is this that answers to his call. ⁵Forgive him as the Christ decides you should, and be His eyes through which you look on him, and speak for Him as well. ⁶He knows the need; the question and the answer. ⁷He will say exactly what to do, in words that you can understand and you can also use. ⁸Do not confuse His function with your own. ⁹He is the Answer. ¹⁰You the one who hears.

6. And what is it He speaks to you about? ²About salvation and the gift of peace. ³About the end of sin and guilt and death. ⁴About the role forgiveness has in Him. ⁵Do you but listen. ⁶For He will be heard by anyone who calls upon His Name, and places his forgiveness in His hands. ⁷Forgiveness has been given Him to teach, to save it from destruction and to make the means for separation, sin and death become again the holy gift of God. ⁸Prayer is His Own right Hand, made free to save as true forgiveness is allowed to come from His eternal vigilance and Love. ⁹Listen and learn, and do not judge. ¹⁰It is to God you turn to hear what you should do. ¹¹His answer will be

clear as morning, nor is His forgiveness what you think it is.

7. Still does He know, and that should be enough. ²Forgiveness has a Teacher Who will fail in nothing. ³Rest a while in this; do not attempt to judge forgiveness, nor to set it in an earthly frame. ⁴Let it arise to Christ, Who welcomes it as gift to Him. ⁵He will not leave you comfortless, nor fail to send His angels down to answer you in His Own Name. ⁶He stands beside the door to which forgiveness is the only key. ⁷Give it to Him to use instead of you, and you will see the door swing silently open upon the shining face of Christ. ⁸Behold your brother there beyond the door; the Son of God as He created him.

3

HEALING

Introduction

1. Prayer has both aids and witnesses which make the steep ascent more gentle and more sure, easing the pain of fear and offering the comfort and the promises of hope. [2]Forgiveness' witness and an aid to prayer, a giver of assurance of success in ultimate attainment of the goal, is healing. [3]Its importance should not be too strongly emphasized, for healing is a sign or symbol of forgiveness' strength, and only an effect or shadow of a change of mind about the goal of prayer.

I. The Cause of Sickness

1. Do not mistake effect for cause, nor think that sickness is apart and separate from what its cause must be. ²It is a sign, a shadow of an evil thought that seems to have reality and to be just, according to the usage of the world. ³It is external proof of inner "sins," and witnesses to unforgiving thoughts that injure and would hurt the Son of God. ⁴Healing the body is impossible, and this is shown by the brief nature of the "cure." ⁵The body yet must die, and so its healing but delays its turning back to dust, where it was born and will return.

2. The body's cause is unforgiveness of the Son of God. ²It has not left its source, and in its pain and aging and the mark of death upon it this is clearly shown. ³Fearful and frail it seems to be to those who think their life is tied to its command and linked to its unstable, tiny breath. ⁴Death stares at them as every moment goes irrevocably past their grasping hands, which cannot hold them back. ⁵And they feel fear as bodies change and sicken. ⁶For they sense the heavy scent of death upon their hearts.

3. The body can be healed as an effect of true forgiveness. ²Only that can give remembrance of immortality, which is the gift of holiness and love. ³Forgiveness must be given

by a mind which understands that it must overlook all shadows on the holy face of Christ, among which sickness should be seen as one. [4]Nothing but that; the sign of judgment made by brother upon brother, and the Son of God upon himself. [5]For he has damned his body as his prison, and forgot that it is he who gave this role to it.

4. What he has done now must God's Son undo. [2]But not alone. [3]For he has thrown away the prison's key; his holy sinlessness and the remembrance of his Father's Love. [4]Yet help is given to him in the Voice his Father placed in him. [5]The power to heal is now his Father's gift, for through His Voice He still can reach His Son, reminding him the body may become his chosen home, but it will never be his home in truth.

5. Distinctions therefore must be made between true healing and its faulty counterpart. [2]The world of opposites is healing's place, for what in Heaven could there be to heal? [3]As prayer within the world can ask amiss and seeming charity forgive to kill, so healing can be false as well as true; a witness to the power of the world or to the everlasting Love of God.

II. False versus True Healing

1. False healing merely makes a poor exchange of one illusion for a "nicer" one; a dream of sickness for a dream of health. ²This can occur at lower forms of prayer, combining with forgiveness kindly meant but not completely understood as yet. ³Only false healing can give way to fear, so sickness will be free to strike again. ⁴False healing can indeed remove a form of pain and sickness. ⁵But the cause remains, and will not lack effects. ⁶The cause is still the wish to die and overcome the Christ. ⁷And with this wish is death a certainty, for prayer *is* answered. ⁸Yet there is a kind of seeming death that has a different source. ⁹It does not come because of hurtful thoughts and raging anger at the universe. ¹⁰It merely signifies the end has come for usefulness of body functioning. ¹¹And so it is discarded as a choice, as one lays by a garment now outworn.

2. This is what death should be; a quiet choice, made joyfully and with a sense of peace, because the body has been kindly used to help the Son of God along the way he goes to God. ²We thank the body, then, for all the service it has given us. ³But we are thankful, too, the need is done to walk the world of limits, and to reach the Christ in hidden forms and clearly seen at most in lovely flashes. ⁴Now

we can behold Him without blinders, in the light that we have learned to look upon again.

3. We call it death, but it is liberty. ²It does not come in forms that seem to be thrust down in pain upon unwilling flesh, but as a gentle welcome to release. ³If there has been true healing, this can be the form in which death comes when it is time to rest a while from labor gladly done and gladly ended. ⁴Now we go in peace to freer air and gentler climate, where it is not hard to see the gifts we gave were saved for us. ⁵For Christ is clearer now; His vision more sustained in us; His Voice, the Word of God, more certainly our own.

4. This gentle passage to a higher prayer, a kind forgiveness of the ways of earth, can only be received with thankfulness. ²Yet first true healing must have come to bless the mind with loving pardon for the sins it dreamed about and laid upon the world. ³Now are its dreams dispelled in quiet rest. ⁴Now its forgiveness comes to heal the world and it is ready to depart in peace, the journey over and the lessons learned.

5. This is not death according to the world, for death is cruel in its frightened eyes and takes the form of punishment for sin. ²How could it be a blessing, then? ³And how could it be welcome when it must be feared? ⁴What heal-

ing has occurred in such a view of what is merely opening the gate to higher prayer and kindly justice done? ⁵Death is reward and not a punishment. ⁶But such a viewpoint must be fostered by the healing that the world cannot conceive. ⁷There is no partial healing. ⁸What but shifts illusions has done nothing. ⁹What is false cannot be partly true. ¹⁰If you are healed your healing is complete. ¹¹Forgiveness is the only gift you give and would receive.

6. False healing rests upon the body's cure, leaving the cause of illness still unchanged, ready to strike again until it brings a cruel death in seeming victory. ²It can be held at bay a little while, and there can be brief respite as it waits to take its vengeance on the Son of God. ³Yet it cannot be overcome until all faith in it has been laid by, and placed upon God's substitute for evil dreams; a world in which there is no veil of sin to keep it dark and comfortless. ⁴At last the gate of Heaven opens and God's Son is free to enter in the home that stands ready to welcome him, and was prepared before time was and still but waits for him.

III. Separation versus Union

1. False healing heals the body in a part, but never as a whole. ²Its separate goals become quite clear in this, for it has not removed the curse of sin that lies on it. ³Therefore it still deceives. ⁴Nor is it made by one who understands the other is exactly like himself. ⁵For it is this that makes true healing possible. ⁶When false, there is some power that another has, not equally bestowed on both as one. ⁷Here is the separation shown. ⁸And here the meaning of true healing has been lost, and idols have arisen to obscure the unity that is the Son of God.

2. Healing-to-separate may seem to be a strange idea. ²And yet it can be said of any form of healing that is based on inequality of any kind. ³These forms may heal the body, and indeed are generally limited to this. ⁴Someone knows better, has been better trained, or is perhaps more talented and wise. ⁵Therefore, he can give healing to the one who stands beneath him in his patronage. ⁶The healing of the body can be done by this because, in dreams, equality cannot be permanent. ⁷The shifts and change are what the dream is made of. ⁸To be healed appears to be to find a wiser one who, by his arts and learning, will succeed.

3. Someone knows better; this the magic phrase by which

the body seems to be the aim of healing as the world conceives of it. ²And to this wiser one another goes to profit by his learning and his skill; to find in him the remedy for pain. ³How can that be? ⁴True healing cannot come from inequality assumed and then accepted as the truth, and used to help restore the wounded and to calm the mind that suffers from the agony of doubt.

4. Is there a role for healing, then, that one can use to offer help for someone else? ²In arrogance the answer must be "no." ³But in humility there is indeed a place for helpers. ⁴It is like the role that helps in prayer, and lets forgiveness be what it is meant to be. ⁵You do not make yourself the bearer of the special gift that brings the healing. ⁶You but recognize your oneness with the one who calls for help. ⁷For in this oneness is his separate sense dispelled, and it is this that made him sick. ⁸There is no point in giving remedy apart from where the source of sickness is, for never thus can it be truly healed.

5. Healers there are, for they are Sons of God who recognize their Source, and understand that all their Source creates is one with them. ²This is the remedy that brings relief which cannot fail. ³It will remain to bless for all eternity. ⁴It heals no part, but wholly and forever. ⁵Now the cause of every malady has been revealed exactly as it

is. ⁶And in that place is written now the holy Word of God. ⁷Sickness and separation must be healed by love and union. ⁸Nothing else can heal as God established healing. ⁹Without Him there is no healing, for there is no love.

6. God's Voice alone can tell you how to heal. ²Listen, and you will never fail to bring His kindly remedy to those He sends to you, to let Him heal them, and to bless all those who serve with Him in healing's name. ³The body's healing will occur because its cause has gone. ⁴And now without a cause, it cannot come again in different form. ⁵Nor will death any more be feared because it has been understood. ⁶There is no fear in one who has been truly healed, for love has entered now where idols used to stand, and fear has given way at last to God.

IV. The Holiness of Healing

1. How holy are the healed! ²For in their sight their brothers share their healing and their love. ³Bringers of peace,—the Holy Spirit's voice, through whom He speaks for God, Whose Voice He is,—such are God's healers. ⁴They but speak for Him and never for themselves. ⁵They have no gifts but those they have from God. ⁶And these

they share because they know that this is what He wills.
[7]They are not special. [8]They are holy. [9]They have chosen
holiness, and given up all separate dreams of special attri-
butes through which they can bestow unequal gifts on
those less fortunate. [10]Their healing has restored their
wholeness so they can forgive, and join the song of prayer
in which the healed sing of their union and their thanks
to God.

2. As witness to forgiveness, aid to prayer, and the effect of
mercy truly taught, healing is blessing. [2]And the world re-
sponds in quickened chorus through the voice of prayer.
[3]Forgiveness shines its merciful reprieve upon each blade
of grass and feathered wing and all the living things upon
the earth. [4]Fear has no haven here, for love has come in all
its holy oneness. [5]Time remains only to let the last embrace of prayer rest on the earth an instant, as the world
is shined away. [6]This instant is the goal of all true healers,
whom the Christ has taught to see His likeness and to
teach like Him.

3. Think what it means to help the Christ to heal! [2]Can
anything be holier than this? [3]God thanks His healers, for
He knows the Cause of healing is Himself, His Love, His
Son, restored as His completion and returned to share
with Him creation's holy joy. [4]Do not ask partial healing,

nor accept an idol for rememberance of Him Whose Love has never changed and never will. ⁵You are as dear to Him as is the whole of His creation, for it lies in you as His eternal gift. ⁶What need have you for shifting dreams within a sorry world? ⁷Do not forget the gratitude of God. ⁸Do not forget the holy grace of prayer. ⁹Do not forget forgiveness of God's Son.

4. You first forgive, then pray, and you are healed. ²Your prayer has risen up and called to God, Who hears and answers. ³You have understood that you forgive and pray but for yourself. ⁴And in this understanding you are healed. ⁵In prayer you have united with your Source, and understood that you have never left. ⁶This level cannot be attained until there is no hatred in your heart, and no desire to attack the Son of God.

5. Never forget this; it is you who are God's Son, and as you choose to be to him so are you to yourself, and God to you. ²Nor will your judgment fail to reach to God, for you will give the role to Him you see in His creation. ³Do not choose amiss, or you will think that it is you who are creator in His place, and He is then no longer Cause but only an effect. ⁴Now healing is impossible, for He is blamed for your deception and your guilt. ⁵He Who is Love becomes

the source of fear, for only fear can now be justified. ⁶Vengeance is His. ⁷His great destroyer, death. ⁸And sickness, suffering and grievous loss become the lot of everyone on earth, which He abandoned to the devil's care, swearing He will deliver it no more.

6. Come unto Me, My children, once again, without such twisted thoughts upon your hearts. ²You still are holy with the Holiness Which fathered you in perfect sinlessness, and still surrounds you with the Arms of peace. ³Dream now of healing. ⁴Then arise and lay all dreaming down forever. ⁵You are he your Father loves, who never left his home, nor wandered in a savage world with feet that bleed, and with a heavy heart made hard against the love that is the truth in you. ⁶Give all your dreams to Christ and let Him be your Guide to healing, leading you in prayer beyond the sorry reaches of the world.

7. He comes for Me and speaks My Word to you. ²I would recall My weary Son to Me from dreams of malice to the sweet embrace of everlasting Love and perfect peace. ³My Arms are open to the Son I love, who does not understand that he is healed, and that his prayers have never ceased to sing his joyful thanks in unison with all creation, in the holiness of Love. ⁴Be still an instant. ⁵Underneath the sounds of harsh and bitter striving and defeat there is a

Voice That speaks to you of Me. ⁶Hear This an instant and you will be healed. ⁷Hear This an instant and you have been saved.

8. Help Me to wake My children from the dream of retribution and a little life beset with fear, that ends so soon it might as well have never been. ²Let Me instead remind you of eternity, in which your joy grows greater as your love extends along with Mine beyond infinity, where time and distance have no meaning. ³While you wait in sorrow Heaven's melody is incomplete, because your song is part of the eternal harmony of love. ⁴Without you is creation unfulfilled. ⁵Return to Me Who never left My Son. ⁶Listen, My child, your Father calls to you. ⁷Do not refuse to hear the Call for Love. ⁸Do not deny to Christ what is His Own. ⁹Heaven is here and Heaven is your home.

9. Creation leans across the bars of time to lift the heavy burden from the world. ²Lift up your hearts to greet its advent. ³See the shadows fade away in gentleness; the thorns fall softly from the bleeding brow of him who is the holy Son of God. ⁴How lovely are you, child of Holiness! ⁵How like to Me! ⁶How lovingly I hold you in My Heart and in My Arms. ⁷How dear is every gift to Me that you have made, who healed My Son and took him from the cross. ⁸Arise and let My thanks be given you.

⁹And with My gratitude will come the gift first of forgiveness, then eternal peace.

10. So now return your holy voice to Me. ²The song of prayer is silent without you. ³The universe is waiting your release because it is its own. ⁴Be kind to it and to yourself, and then be kind to Me. ⁵I ask but this; that you be comforted and live no more in terror and in pain. ⁶Do not abandon Love. ⁷Remember this; whatever you may think about yourself, whatever you may think about the world, your Father needs you and will call to you until you come to Him in peace at last.